Which Way ARE *WE* TRAVELING?

CHUCK HAYES

Editing, cover design, and page formatting by ChristianEditingServices.com.
Cover photo: Martine De Graaf | Dreamstime.com

ISBN 978-0-615-95820-0

Printed in the United States of America.

CONTENTS

PREFACE

While imprisoned, John Bunyan penned one of the most famous and sought-after books outside the Bible. Usually known simply as *The Pilgrim's Progress*, the full title is *The Pilgrim's Progress from This World to That Which Is to Come; Delivered under the Similitude of a Dream*. In Bunyan's dream, he sees Christian, an everyman character who is greatly burdened in his soul. Unable to persuade his wife and children of the coming judgment he foresees, he forsakes all to save himself. His actions remind us of Jesus' words: "So likewise, whoever of you does not forsake all that he has cannot be My disciple" (Luke 14:33).

Traveling from the "City of Destruction" to the "Celestial City," Christian and his temporary companions Formalist and Hypocrisy come to the foot of "Hill Difficulty," which is steep and high. Formalist and Hypocrisy, seeing that there appear to be easier ways to the same destination than this narrow way up the hill, make a decision that has dangerous and destructive consequences. Christian, on the other hand, decides to go up the narrow hill, saying this:

> "The hill, though high, I covet to ascend, The difficulty will not me offend; For I perceive the way to life lies here. Come, pluck up heart, let's neither faint nor fear; Better, though difficult, the right way to go, Than wrong, though easy, where the end is woe."[1]

What about You and Me?

Many professing Christians today, especially in the West, seem to have the idea that health, wealth, and prosperity should characterize those who travel the narrow way, following Jesus. In fact, this false teaching regularly emanates from "prosperity preachers." But has mainstream evangelicalism bought into this easy-life teaching as well? Recently, my wife and I visited a church where the fifteen-minute sermon was about how "good Christians" and "good church members" are blessed by God. Obviously, we are all recipients of God's innumerable blessings, and the psalmist David rightly declared, "Bless the Lord, O my soul, and forget not all His benefits" (Psalm 103:2). Yet, the way to heaven is paved with joyful suffering! The whole idea that we can enjoy an easy life void of tribulations, distresses, and persecutions because of union with Christ is contrary to Jesus' teaching. He said, "Whoever desires to come after Me, let him deny himself, and take up his cross, and follow Me. For whoever desires to save his life will lose it, but whoever loses his life for My sake and the gospel's will save it" (Mark 8:34-35).

What about you and me? Are we like Formalist and Hypocrisy, trusting in laws and ordinances? Or can we say with Christian, "I walk by the rule of my Master"? Are we like Formalist and Hypocrisy, who travel the easy way? Or can we say with Christian, "The hill, though high, I covet to ascend, The difficulty will not me offend; For I perceive the way to life lies here"? Which way are *we* traveling? I think you would agree that our answer has eternal implications.

A Command and a Warning

At the close of the Sermon on the Mount, Jesus presses His hearers for a decision to enter a gate that is narrow, though difficult, while warning of the consequences of traveling the easy, more popular way. And He punctuates His challenge by saying that only few find the narrow way, whereas many who are certain Jesus is their Lord find out in the end they were eternally wrong. This is what Jesus says.

> Enter by the narrow gate; for wide is the gate and broad is the way that leads to destruction, and there are many who go in by it. Because narrow is the gate and difficult is the way which leads to life, and there are few who find it.
>
> – MATTHEW 7:13-14

The purpose of this book is twofold. First, my desire is an evangelistic one. I want to demonstrate from the Scriptures that an easy life and religion is a deceived life that ultimately ends in destruction, and I want to plead with you to "enter by the narrow gate." Second, I desire to encourage suffering saints who are currently traveling the narrow way. So, join me in the pages that follow, remembering, "Better, though difficult, the right way to go, Than wrong, though easy, where the end is woe."

CHAPTER 1

THE IMPOSSIBILITY OF ENTERING THE KINGDOM BY WORKS OF THE LAW

*S*eeing the multitudes, Jesus began the first of His five major discourses recorded in Matthew. This one, commonly known as the Sermon on the Mount, focuses on the nature of the kingdom of heaven. His audience, made up of His disciples and other curious listeners, heard Him pronounce the impossibility of entering heaven by one's outward righteousness and traditions and set forth the fundamental principles His true followers are to live out by His grace through the ages. While there are various interpretations of Matthew 5–7, I think it's safe to say that this magnificent sermon is both evangelistic and the standard by which Christians are to conduct their lives as the "salt of the earth" and the "light of the world."

WE ARE ALL GUILTY AND LOST

Jesus began with the Beatitudes, a series of statements introduced by the words "Blessed are" (Matthew 5:1-12), which describe the happiness of those who belong to the kingdom of heaven. Jesus then said something shocking: "For I say to you, that unless your righteousness exceeds the righteousness of the scribes and

Pharisees, you will by no means enter the kingdom of heaven" (Matthew 5:20). This was startling because these religious Jews were, in the minds of nearly everyone, models of righteousness. And if the outward, legalistic righteousness of the scribes and Pharisees was not enough to get them into the kingdom of heaven, how could anyone enter the kingdom? This was exactly Jesus' point. No matter how sincere or zealous one is toward God, no one will enter heaven by the works of the law.

> Now we know that whatever the law says it speaks to those who are under the law, so that every mouth may be stopped, and the whole world may be held accountable to God. For by *works of the law* no human being will be justified in his sight, since through the law comes knowledge of sin.
>
> — ROMANS 3:19-20 ESV (EMPHASIS ADDED)

We are *all* under the law. The Jews have the "oracles of God" (Romans 3:2), whereas the Gentiles (non-Jews) have the works of the law written on their hearts (Romans 2:15). And since we are under the law, we are all under sin, "being filled with all unrighteousness, sexual immorality, wickedness, covetousness, maliciousness; full of envy, murder, strife, deceit, evil-mindedness; … whisperers, backbiters, haters of God, violent, proud, boasters, inventors of evil things, disobedient to parents, undiscerning, untrustworthy, unloving, unforgiving, unmerciful; who, knowing the righteous judgment of God, that those who practice such things are deserving of death, not only do the same but also approve of those who practice them" (Romans 1:29-32). Since we cannot perfectly keep the law of God, that law exposes our sinful hearts; and we have no choice but to quickly put our hands over our mouths so as to stop any and all excuses. We must admit that we are *all* guilty and lost! No amount of good works can obtain for us a right standing with God.

10

THE LAW AND OUR SIN

Later, in Romans 7, the apostle Paul shared his personal encounter with the law.

> What shall we say then? Is the law sin? Certainly not! On the contrary, I would not have known sin except through the law. For I would not have known covetousness unless the law had said, "You shall not covet." But sin, taking opportunity by the commandment, produced in me all manner of evil desire. For apart from the law sin was dead. I was alive once without the law, but when the commandment came, sin revived and I died. And the commandment, which was to bring life, I found to bring death. For sin, taking occasion by the commandment, deceived me, and by it killed me. Therefore the law is holy, and the commandment holy and just and good.
>
> – ROMANS 7:7-12

Paul had been convinced that he was acceptable to God because of his own righteousness; that is, by his outward religiosity and efforts to keep the commandments. But here he admitted that the law, which he thought brought life, instead exposed his sin. "For I would not have known covetousness unless the law had said, 'You shall not covet.'" Likewise, we would not know lying, stealing, and using God's name in vain were sins had the law not said, "You shall not bear false witness" (Exodus 20:16), "You shall not steal" (Exodus 20:15), and "You shall not take the name of the Lord your God in vain" (Exodus 20:7). In and of itself, the law is not sinful but holy, reflecting God's character. Nevertheless, any and all attempts to meet the perfect requirements of the law and thus attain salvation bring about a curse because our efforts to keep the law always fall short of perfection (Galatians 3:10). Like Paul before his conversion, many today are deceived into thinking *their efforts* to keep the commandments will somehow deliver them from the terrors of hell. Yet the more we try to keep the commandments, the more we reveal our just condemnation.

THE GREAT COMMANDMENT

When Jesus was asked what the great commandment of the law was, He said this.

> "'You shall love the Lord your God with all your heart, with all your soul, and with all your mind.' This is the first and great commandment. And the second is like it: 'You shall love your neighbor as yourself.' On these two commandments hang all the Law and the Prophets."
>
> — MATTHEW 22:37-40

The summation of the Old Testament (the Law and the Prophets) is love—love for God and love for our neighbor. The greatest of man's religious duty is to love God and others in "the most sincere, upright, and perfect manner."[2]

When a certain lawyer stood up and questioned Jesus about eternal life, Jesus said, "What is written in the law? What is your reading of it?" (Luke 10:26). The man answered by referencing Deuteronomy 6:5 (love God) and Leviticus 19:18 (love your neighbor). Then Jesus answered, "You have answered rightly; do this and you will live" (Luke 10:28). If the lawyer truly, perfectly loved both God and his fellow man, as he was obligated to do, he would live. If you and I love God and others in "the most sincere, upright, and perfect manner," as we are obligated to do, we will live. However, we already have indicated that all our efforts to obey God fall short; they are imperfect and futile. Indeed, if we think we can get to heaven through our own flawed efforts, Jesus' descent from heaven, His birth, His suffering, and His death were all in vain. Paul declared, "I do not set aside the grace of God; for if righteousness comes through the law, then Christ died in vain" (Galatians 2:21).

So we conclude with the great apostle that "all have sinned and fall short of the glory of God" (Romans 3:23). Therefore, it is impossible to enter the kingdom (heaven) by works of the law. How, then, can we be made right with God? How can we be freed from the law of sin and death? If we can't enter through the narrow gate by works, then how? I think you would agree that we need some good news!

CHAPTER 2

The Person of Jesus Christ, His Mission, and His Return

*J*esus Christ, the only begotten Son of God, is the divinely appointed mediator between God and man. Having taken upon Himself human nature, yet without sin, He perfectly fulfilled the law, suffered and died upon the cross for the salvation of sinners. He was buried, and rose again the third day, and ascended to His Father, at whose hand He ever liveth to make intercession for His people. He is the only Mediator, the Prophet, Priest and King of the Church, and Sovereign of the Universe.

– James P. Boyce

His Deity

John, the last living apostle, opens his gospel with a fascinating truth regarding the person of Christ. "In the beginning was the Word, and the Word was with God, and the Word was God" (John 1:1). When John says, "In the beginning," our thoughts immediately take us back to Genesis 1:1, where the heavens and the earth were created. But John informs his readers, "In the beginning was the Word." Even before the heavens and earth were created, Jesus, the Word (*logos*), *was*. John wastes no time in revealing the truth that the Word already existed before the creation of the universe, thereby rejecting a host of heresies concerning the person of Christ that have plagued the church throughout its history. Such false teaching, by the way, is the reason for the early creeds and confessions. The saying, "No creed but the Bible," sounds very spiritual, but false prophets and false teachers have always twisted the Scriptures to their own fancy.

Next, John says, "The Word was with God." Before creation, Jesus Christ, the Word of God, was face to face with God the Father in perfect fellowship that was "rich and glorious, filled with infinite delight and serene blessedness."[3] In Jesus' High Priestly Prayer, He said, "And now, O Father, glorify Me together with Yourself, with the glory which I had with You before the world was" (John 17:5). This intimate relationship was not just between the Father and Son but also was a Trinitarian relationship the Father, Son, and Holy Spirit enjoyed "before the world was."

John closes his opening statement with, "The Word was God." Jesus is God (deity)! In his book John will continue to unpack this glorious truth through Jesus' miracles, signs and wonders, and seven metaphoric "I AM" statements.

- "I am the bread of life" (John 6:35).

- "I am the light of the world" (John 8:12).

- "I am the door of the sheep" (John 10:7; see also John 10:9).

- "I am the good shepherd" (John 10:11, 14).

- "I am the resurrection and the life" (John 11:25).

- "I am the way, the truth, and the life" (John 14:6).

- "I am the true vine" (John 15:1).

In each of these statements, the Greek expression (*ego eimi*) is a reference to the God of the Old Testament, who revealed Himself to Moses as "I AM" (Exodus 3:14). Applied to Jesus, these statements are clear indicators of His deity. In addition to the "I am" statements above, we find Jesus responding to the Jews who wanted to know who He was, by saying, "Most assuredly, I say to you, before Abraham was, I AM" (John 8:58). They knew exactly what He meant because they took up stones to throw at Him. Again, when Philip said to Jesus, "Lord, show us the Father, and it is sufficient for us" (John 14:8), Jesus responded, "Have I been with you so long, and yet you have not known Me, Philip? He who has seen Me has seen the Father; so how can you say, 'Show us the Father'?" (John 14:9). To see and experience Jesus was to encounter God. One of the strongest arguments supporting the deity of Christ is found when Thomas wanted visual proof of Jesus' resurrection because he was not with the other disciples when Jesus first appeared to them. Jesus stood in their midst and told Thomas, "Reach your finger here, and look at My hands; and reach your hand here, and put it into My side. Do not be unbelieving, but believing" (John 20:27). Thomas answered, "My Lord and My God!" (v. 28). Thomas's clear declaration that Jesus is God was not refuted but accepted by the Lord.

HIS HUMANITY

One of the greatest events in history is recorded in John's gospel: "And the Word became flesh and dwelt among us, and we beheld His glory, the glory as of the only begotten of the Father, full of grace and truth" (John 1:14). The eternal, preexistent Son of God "emptied Himself of His privileges" (NKJV footnote), was born of a virgin (otherwise He would have inherited Adam's sin), and became man. How wonderfully profound is that? Although He was fully human, He remained fully God. John Philips observes, "He did not cease to be God, the second person of the godhead at his incarnation, God the Son; but at the same time his humanity was both real and complete."[4] Thus, Jesus Christ has two natures—divine and human—united in one person.

These two natures are clearly portrayed in Paul's letter to the church at Colosse, when he writes, "For in him the whole fullness of deity dwells bodily" (Colossians 2:9 ESV). While maintaining the attributes of deity—authority, power, grace, and truth—Jesus was a historical human being who lived out His life on the world's stage. The totality of God was visible in the body of Jesus Christ.

Jesus "dwelt," or literally "tabernacled," among the people. This is a clear allusion to the Old Testament tabernacle, where God met with His people. Those among whom He dwelt "beheld His glory." The word *glory* reminds us of the *shekinah* glory, that cloud that filled the temple, indicating God's presence (Exod. 40:34). Thus, when the people looked upon the unique, one-of-a-kind Son of God, they observed Jesus as fully God and fully Man.

HIS MISSION

Yes, it was Jesus' mission to heal the brokenhearted, give sight to the blind, raise the dead, and set free those who were oppressed; and, of course, it was also His mission to "seek and to save that which was lost" (Luke 19:10). Ultimately, however, *His mission was to suffer and die!* "And He began to teach them that the Son of Man *must* suffer many things, and be rejected by the elders and chief priests and scribes, and be killed, and after three days rise again" (Mark 8:31, emphasis mine).

The key word here is *must*. Elsewhere, when speaking of His death, Jesus said, "And as Moses lifted up the serpent in the wilderness, even so *must* the Son of Man be lifted up" (John 3:14, emphasis mine). This was His mission. Jesus *must* suffer and die and rise three days later. But why?

HIS BEARING SIN

Nothing we *do* can make us right with God, as we showed in chapter 1. Therefore, we are unable to atone, or adequately pay, for our sins! On that old rugged cross, Jesus, the Lamb of God, suffered and died to take away the sin of the world. John the Baptist declared, "Behold! The Lamb of God who takes away the sin of the world" (John 1:29)! Similarly, Peter wrote that Christ "Himself bore our sins in His own body on the tree" (1 Peter 2:24). The wonderful hymn by Robert Lowry, "Nothing but the Blood," eloquently expresses this great truth.

> Nothing can for sin atone,
> Nothing but the blood of Jesus;
> Naught of good that I have done,
> Nothing but the blood of Jesus.

The blood of sacrificial lambs was regularly offered to the Lord in the Old Testament—at Passover (Exodus 12:1-28), during daily offerings (Numbers 28:4), and at other times. Isaiah 53:7 pictures Christ as the sacrificial Lamb, stating, "He was oppressed and He was afflicted, yet He opened not His mouth; He was led as a lamb to the slaughter, and as a sheep before its shearers is silent, so He opened not His mouth." If John the Baptist had the Passover in mind when he declared Jesus the Lamb of God, it certainly was an appropriate picture, for not just any lamb could be used for the Passover. In giving instructions for the Passover, God told His people, "Your lamb shall be without blemish" (Exodus 12:5). It had to be perfect! Peter says it like this: "You were not redeemed with corruptible things, like silver or gold, from your aimless conduct received by tradition from your fathers, but with the precious blood of Christ, as of a lamb without blemish and without spot" (1 Peter 1:18-19). Hence, the ongoing sacrifice of perfect lambs offered in the Old Testament prefigured the perfect, sinless Lamb of God, who, as the Sin-Bearer, would take

19

away the sin of the world once for all—for those of every tribe, tongue, people, and nation.

HIS BEARING WRATH

Before we move on, it is important to look more closely at what Jesus accomplished on the cross. Four times in the New Testament, the word *propitiation* is used (Romans 3:25; Hebrews 2:17; 1 John 2:2; 4:10). *Propitiation* has the meaning of satisfying, or appeasing, God's wrath. *The New Bible Dictionary* says, "Propitiation properly signifies the removal of wrath by the offering of a gift."[5] In many places the Bible speaks of God's wrath toward sinners (see John 3:36; Romans 1:18; 5:9; 1 Thessalonians 1:10). Jesus willingly offered His life on the cross to satisfy the wrath of God against sin. Jesus drank the full cup of God's wrath! This is why He cried out, "My God, My God, why have You forsaken Me?" (Matthew 27:46). Thus, Jesus is both the Sin-Bearer and the Wrath-Bearer.

We (mankind) did not love God. Our sinful lives gave testimony to the fact that we lived for ourselves and the attractions and pleasures the world and the Devil offered us. But despite our being sinners who fell short of God's glory, He demonstrated His love toward us by sending His Son, the eternal, preexistent Word, who became Man, born of the Virgin Mary, and lived among us. Those who looked upon Him saw the "brightness of His glory" (Hebrews 1:3) and the attributes of Deity. His mission was clear: He must suffer and die! The God-Man offered His life on the cross to bear the wrath of God and to bear the sins of those of every tribe, tongue, people, and nation.

> "Worthy is the Lamb who was slain to receive power and riches and wisdom, and strength and honor and glory and blessing!"
>
> — REVELATION 5:12

HIS RESURRECTION

That early Sunday morning following the crucifixion of Jesus, several women came to the tomb where His body had been buried. When they arrived, the large stone covering the tomb's entrance had been rolled away and the body of Jesus was gone. Then two angels, who appeared as men in shining garments, said, "Why do you seek the living among the dead? He is not here, but is risen!" (Luke 24:5-6). Jesus was alive, and He soon was seen by Mary Magdalene (John 20:11-18) and the other women (Matthew 28:9-10); Peter, James, and the apostles (1 Corinthians 15:5, 7); the two disciples on the way to Emmaus (Luke 24:13-35); and five hundred others (1 Corinthians 15:6). And, finally, after His ascension, He was seen by Paul (1 Corinthians 15:8). The resurrection is indeed a historical fact!

In His resurrection, Jesus defeated sin, our greatest enemy death, and the works of the devil. But His resurrection also signaled the Father's approval and acceptance of His Son's suffering and death as the Sin-Bearer and Wrath-Bearer. Hence, forgiveness, peace, and righteousness are secured for the Christian (Romans 4:25).

The resurrection of the Lord Jesus also guarantees our final victory and future resurrection.

> Now this I say, brethren, that flesh and blood cannot inherit the kingdom of God; nor does corruption inherit incorruption. Behold, I tell you a mystery: We shall not all sleep, but we shall all be changed—in a moment, in the twinkling of an eye, at the last trumpet. For the trumpet will sound, and the dead will be raised incorruptible, and we shall be changed. For this corruptible must put on incorruption, and this mortal must put on immortality. So when this corruptible has put on incorruption, and this mortal has put on immortality, then shall be brought to

21

pass the saying that is written: "Death is swallowed up in victory. O Death, where is your sting? O Hades, where is your victory?" The sting of death is sin, and the strength of sin is the law. But thanks be to God, who gives us the victory through our Lord Jesus Christ.

– 1 CORINTHIANS 15:50-57

HIS ASCENSION

After the resurrection, Jesus ascended into heaven. "Now when He had spoken these things, while they watched, He was taken up, and a cloud received Him out of their sight" (Acts 1:9). Now at the right hand of the Father, He always lives to make intercession for us (Romans 8:34; Hebrews 7:25). When we sin, He is our advocate (1 John 2:1). When we hurt and have needs, we have a sympathetic high priest who understands (Hebrews 4:15).

HIS RETURN

Just as Jesus ascended into heaven, one day He will return from heaven. "And while they looked steadfastly toward heaven as He went up, behold, two men stood by them in white apparel, who also said, 'Men of Galilee, why do you stand gazing up into heaven? This same Jesus, who was taken up from you into heaven, will so come in like manner as you saw Him go into heaven'" (Acts 1:10-11). One day, history as we know it will end!

The Bible reveals that prior to the return of Christ certain signs will occur.

- ◆ There will be wars and rumors of wars (Matthew 24:6).

- ◆ Nation will rise against nation (Matthew 24:7).

- There will be famines, pestilences, and earthquakes (Matthew 24:7).

- The gospel will be preached to all the nations (Matthew 24:14).

- False christs and false prophets will arise (Matthew 24:24).

- The sun will be darkened, the moon will not give light, and the stars will fall from heaven (Matthew 24:29).

- There will be a falling away, and the man of sin will be revealed (2 Thessalonians 2:3).

The Son of Man will come on the clouds of heaven with power and glory (Matthew 24:30). He will consume the lawless one, "with the breath of His mouth" (2 Thessalonians 2:8), raise the dead (John 5:28-29), execute judgment (John 5:22, 27; Revelation 20:11-15), and make all things new (Revelation 21:5).

IT IS DONE

And He said to me, "It is done! I am the Alpha and the Omega, the Beginning and the End. I will give of the fountain of the water of life freely to him who thirsts. He who overcomes shall inherit all things, and I will be his God and he shall be My son."

— REVELATION 21:6-7

CHAPTER 3

ENTER BY THE NARROW GATE

*O*h, how we ought to search our hearts here today. Have I come to this place of total commitment in my life? Have I yielded my life to the sovereign lordship of Him who dies upon the cross for me? I want you to know that the gates of paradise have been swung open to you. The narrow gate is open … if you will take a step of faith and come through this narrow gate, and commit your life to Him. … He also says, "him who comes unto Me I will in no wise cast out."

— STEVEN LAWSON

RIGHTEOUSNESS FROM GOD

As we saw in chapter 1, the law given through Moses, though it was "holy and just and good," exposed our guilt and sin, rendering the whole world accountable to God and without excuse. Furthermore, because our hearts are sinful, no one will be justified (declared righteous) by the works of the law. So, we concluded that we were in desperate need of some good news.

Chapter 2 revealed that the good news came in the person of Jesus Christ, who eternally existed with God the Father and God the Holy Spirit in perfect fellowship "before the world was." Jesus, the Word of God, became Man and lived among people with all the divine attributes shining forth in the "brightness of His glory" (Hebrews 1:3), full of grace and truth. As He went about doing good, His mission was clear: He would shed His blood as the Sin-Bearer and Wrath-Bearer for those from every tribe, tongue, people, and nation so that they might forever worship the Lamb that was slain.

Now that we understand man's plight and the good news, we must turn to Jesus' words: "Enter by the narrow gate" (Matthew 7:13). There is no other way to enter the kingdom of heaven! If our righteousness is to exceed that of the scribes and Pharisees (Matthew 5:20), then we must stop laboring to enter by works of the law, as they did, and submit to the righteousness that comes from God. Paul spoke of this when he wrote of being in Christ.

> Not having my own righteousness, which is from the law, but that which is through faith in Christ, the righteousness which is from God by faith.
>
> — PHILIPPIANS 3:9

Paul had an impressive resume: He was "circumcised the eighth day, of the stock of Israel, of the tribe of Benjamin, a Hebrew of the Hebrews; concerning the law, a Pharisee; concerning zeal, persecuting the church; concerning the righteousness which is in the law, blameless" (Philippians 3:5-6). Perhaps, like Paul, you too can list some impressive accomplishments: baptized when you were young, a long-standing church member, sang in the choir, taught Sunday school or led a small group, lived a morally upright life! Yet, as significant as these things are, they cannot give us a right standing with God. By the grace of God, Paul could look back on his accomplishments and heritage and say,

"But what things were gain to me, these I have counted loss for Christ" (Philippians 3:7). He admitted that his impressive religious resume (what things were gain) was actually rubbish (loss) compared to the "knowledge of Christ Jesus [his] Lord" (Philippians 3:8). Like Paul, you must abandon any and all dependence on human merit and works of the law and submit to the righteousness that comes from God through repentance and faith in Christ. The things mentioned above—baptism, church membership, teaching, and a moral lifestyle—will naturally flow from your new life in Christ, but they can never save.

REPENTANCE

After four hundred years of silence following the close of the Old Testament era, John the Baptist appeared, preparing the way of the Lord and saying, "Repent, for the kingdom of heaven is at hand!" (Matthew 3:2). Likewise, at the beginning of Jesus' earthly ministry, He said, "The time is fulfilled, and the kingdom of God is at hand. Repent, and believe in the gospel" (Mark 1:15). When the Twelve were sent out, they "preached that people should repent" (Mark 6:12). Following Pentecost, Peter said, "Repent therefore and be converted, that your sins may be blotted out, so that times of refreshing may come from the presence of the Lord" (Acts 3:19). And in Athens Paul proclaimed, "Truly, these times of ignorance God overlooked, but now commands all men everywhere to repent" (Acts 17:30). As we can see, repentance is necessary for salvation!

What does repentance mean? Repentance is turning from sin and to Christ—it is a change of mind and a change of direction. In our sin we are all naturally going in the same direction. When we hear the good news, however, the Holy Spirit convicts us of sorrow over our sin (John 16:8-11). Spurgeon said of repentance, "There must be sorrow for sin and hatred of it in true repentance, or else I have read my Bible to little purpose."[6] To the Corinthians, Paul wrote, "For godly sorrow produces repentance leading to salvation, not to be regretted; but the sorrow of the world produces death" (2 Corinthians 7:10). There is a sorrow that produces repentance, and there is a sorrow that produces death. What is the difference? Godly sorrow is the conviction that our sins are against God; it is a deep sorrow that leads us to turn from our sins to the Savior, Jesus Christ. Worldly sorrow is simply sorrow over getting caught. This kind of sorrow leads to death and eternal judgment. Spurgeon is right: "There must be sorrow for sin and hatred of it in true repentance."

FAITH

Inseparable from repentance is faith. The Christian Apologetics and Research Ministry (CARM) offers this helpful definition.

> "Now faith is the assurance of things hoped for, the conviction of things not seen" (Heb. 11:1). Faith should be understood as synonymous with trust and or confidence in something. Within Christianity, it is a divine gift (Rom. 12:3) and comes by hearing the Word of God (Rom. 10:17). It is the means by which the grace of God is accounted to the believer who trusts in the work of Jesus on the cross (Eph. 2:8). Without faith it is impossible to please God (Heb. 11:6). It is by faith that Christians live their lives, "The righteous shall live by faith," (Hab. 2:4; Rom. 1:17).[7]

Faith, then, is the instrument, or means, whereby we are justified, or declared righteous, before God. Paul wrote, "Therefore we conclude that a man is justified by faith apart from the deeds of the law" (Romans 3:28); and, "By grace you have been saved through faith, and that not of yourselves; it is the gift of God, not of works, lest anyone should boast" (Ephesians 2:8-9). With godly sorrow, the believer repents and trusts (has faith) in the work of Jesus on the cross!

Yet faith is also "the gift of God." Faith does not lay dormant in each and every one of us, just waiting to be awakened. Upon hearing the word of truth, the gospel, the Spirit of God "quickens," or "makes alive," sinners, leading them to repent and believe. Paul also speaks elsewhere of faith being a gift, writing, "For to you it has been granted on behalf of Christ, not only to believe in Him, but also to suffer for His sake" (Philippians 1:29). Contrary to popular belief, both faith and suffering are gifts. The word translated "granted" means "to give freely."[8] Therefore, both salvation and suffering (we will discuss suffering in greater detail in the following chapters) are gifts of grace to God's people.

Faith, of course, is set apart from works: "Not of works, lest anyone should boast." If we could be justified by works, then we would boast about our accomplishment, right? "For if Abraham was justified by works, he has something to boast about, but not before God" (Romans 4:2). If entrance into heaven could be gained by works, those who attained it could boast about it, and God actually would owe them salvation. "Now to him who works, the wages are not accounted as grace but as debt" (Romans 4:4). But Scripture is clear: "Abraham believed God, and it was accounted to him for righteousness" (Romans 4:3). We are justified by repentant faith, not by works.

IN CHRIST ALONE

When Peter preached his famous sermon on the day of Pentecost, the people were "cut to the heart" and said, "Men and brethren, what shall we do?" (Acts 2:37). Similarly, when Paul and Silas were imprisoned, the jailer asked them, "Sirs, what must I do to be saved?" (Acts 16:30). And maybe as you are reading this little booklet, you are asking the same thing: "What must I do?" The answer is simple: Enter by the narrow gate through repentance and faith! Turn away from your sin and believe in Christ alone, who perfectly fulfilled the law, "humbled Himself and became obedient to the point of death, even the death of the cross" (Philippians 2:8).

CHAPTER 4

COUNTING THE COST

I grant freely that it costs little to be a mere outward Christian. A man has only got to attend a place of worship twice on Sunday, and to be tolerably moral during the week, and he has gone as far as thousands around him ever go in religion. All this is cheap and easy work: it entails no self-denial or self-sacrifice. If this is saving Christianity, and it will take us to heaven when we die, we must alter the description of the way of life, and write, "Wide is the gate and broad is the way that leads to heaven!"

But it does cost something to be a real Christian, according to the standard of the Bible. There are enemies to be overcome, battles to be fought, sacrifices to be made, an Egypt to be forsaken, a wilderness to be passed through, a cross to be carried, a race to be run. Conversion is not putting a man in an arm-chair and taking him easily to heaven. It is the beginning of a mighty conflict, in which it costs much to win the victory. Hence arises the unspeakable importance of "counting the cost."

– J. C. RYLE

THE COST – DENY YOURSELF

Entrance through the narrow gate requires repentance and faith. But we should not make a hasty decision without first counting the cost. Indeed, Jesus Himself warned that we should consider the cost of following Him, so it is appropriate to include a chapter on this subject. *To be clear, the terms Jesus set forth for following Him are not works; rather, they explain the meaning of genuine faith in Him.* After observing what it looks like to trust and follow Christ, we will be better equipped to settle the question, "Which way are *we* traveling?"

Often, when multitudes gathered about Jesus for various reasons, He would turn to them and invite them to follow Him. Yet He set the cost of following Him so high that only few would accept His terms. He said, "Whoever desires to come after Me, let him deny himself, and take up his cross, and follow Me" (Mark 8:34). Are you ready to follow Jesus? Then you must deny yourself. Jesus demands of us what we naturally can't and don't want to do. He essentially says we must let go of all self-righteousness, traditions, and religion we would otherwise rely on for salvation. We must count all things as rubbish (loss) for Christ!

THE COST – TAKE UP YOUR CROSS

Next, we must take up a cross. In Jesus' day, the people knew full well what He meant when He spoke of a cross—it meant execution. David Platt offers this. "Now this is taking it to another level. *Pick up an instrument of torture and follow me.* This is getting plain weird ... and kind of creepy. Imagine a leader coming on the scene today and inviting all who would come after him to pick up an electric chair and become his disciple. Any takers?"[9] To take up a cross is to submit to suffering, shame, and possible martyrdom for Jesus' sake; and this is very unpopular, especially in places where prosperity rules the day.

THE COST – FOLLOW ME

Many times Jesus said, "Follow Me." He was demanding complete abandonment to His lordship, calling on people to trust and obey Him, to love and adore Him, and to treasure Him more than family and friends, possessions, and even life itself. Have you left all to follow Him to receive all you need in Him? Peter said to Jesus, "See, we have left all and followed You. Therefore what shall we have?" (Matthew 19:27). Jesus said this.

> "Assuredly I say to you, that in the regeneration, when the Son of Man sits on the throne of His glory, you who have followed Me will also sit on twelve thrones, judging the twelve tribes of Israel. And everyone who has left houses or brothers or sisters or father or mother or wife or children or lands, for My name's sake, shall receive a hundredfold, and inherit eternal life."
>
> — MATTHEW 19:28-29

Those who leave all to follow Jesus will not be disappointed!

THE COST – COMFORT

As Jesus traveled along a road, someone said to Him, "Lord, I will follow You wherever You go" (Luke 9:57). I just had to stop and ponder this impulsive statement before I wrote any further.

33

Many people, like this man, have made quick and impulsive decisions to follow Christ without counting the cost. And maybe you, dear reader, have done the same. That is, you are content to be a mere "outward Christian" and you never considered what Jesus demands of you. You attend church and maintain a moral lifestyle, but that is as far as it goes for you. Your Christianity is easy! Ryle alluded to the fact that "thousands" do the same. I would venture to say millions! Jesus, however, told the man who expressed a desire to follow Him, "Foxes have holes and birds of the air have nests, but the Son of Man has nowhere to lay His head" (Luke 9:58). Without counting the cost, it's easy to say, "Lord, I will follow you wherever You go." But what does following Him, having true faith in Him, look like? Have we sat down with a Bible in our hands and considered the words of our Lord? Are we willing to follow Jesus under these radical conditions?

Jesus informed potential followers that if they want to live comfortably in this world and follow Him at the same time, then eternal life is not for them. Jesus said, "For whoever desires to save his life will lose it, but whoever loses his life for My sake will save it" (Luke 9:24). Those who want an easy, comfortable Christianity (to save their lives) will find out in the end that hell will swallow them up (they will lose their lives).

THE COST – POSSESSIONS

Then Jesus said to another man, "Follow Me" (Luke 9:59). But the man replied, "Lord, let me first go and bury my father." This man implied that he wanted his father's inheritance. If the man heard Jesus' earlier response (v. 58), he probably thought he would need some extra spending money. But, like comfort, money is a stumbling block. A rich young ruler was sincere about eternal life, but Jesus said to him, "You still lack one thing. Sell all that you have and distribute to the poor, and you will have treasure in heaven; and come, follow Me" (Luke 18:22). Instead of leaving all to follow Jesus, the man became sorrowful, because he had great possessions. He loved his stuff more than he loved Jesus.

Often, those of us in the West allow our culture and its materialism to interfere with our interpretation of Scripture, and we water down Jesus' words. For example, Jesus said, "So likewise, whoever of you does not forsake all that he has cannot be My disciple" (Luke 14:33). The Holman Christian Standard Bible (HCSB) translation reads, "In the same way, therefore, every one of you who does not say good-bye to all his possessions cannot be My disciple." We might read that text and think, "Well, He doesn't really mean forsake *all*." However, if we look at the actions of the early church, we see how they understood Jesus' words. We read in Acts 2, "Now all who believed were together, and had all things in common, and sold their possessions and goods, and divided them among all, as anyone had need" (vv. 44-45). Likewise, in chapter 4 of Acts we find this: "Nor was there anyone among them who lacked; for all who were possessors of lands or houses sold them, and brought the proceeds of the things that were sold, and laid them at the apostles' feet; and they distributed to each as anyone had need" (vv. 34-35). This is tough. Jesus is not saying we can't have homes, transportation, or bank accounts, but He is saying our possessions must not possess us. We are to travel lightly while holding on to our possessions loosely, ready to forsake them if necessary to meet the needs of others. Jesus responded to the man who wanted his inheritance by saying, "Let the dead bury their own dead, but you go and preach the kingdom of God" (Luke 9:60). Preaching the good news was the top priority! Nothing is to hinder immediate obedience, even if it means suffering discomfort, forsaking possessions, or devaluing our nearest and dearest relationships.

THE COST – RELATIONSHIPS

Still another person said to Jesus, "Lord, I will follow You, but let me first go and bid them farewell who are at my house" (Luke 9:61). Okay, surely Jesus would let this poor soul say good-bye to his family, right? Nope! Jesus said, "No one, having put his hand to the plow, and looking back, is fit for the kingdom of God" (Luke 9:62). Our love for family and friends should be like hate when compared to our love for Jesus. A sweet, ninety-seven-year-old lady asked me after services one Thursday evening, "Do we really have to love Jesus more than family?" Of course, I said yes, and I read this text to her: "If anyone comes to Me and does not hate his father and mother, wife and children, brothers and sisters, yes, and his own life also, he cannot be My disciple. And whoever does not bear his cross and come after Me cannot be My disciple" (Luke 14:26-27). If we love Jesus less than we love others, we cannot be Christians. Of course, we always want to be balanced. Jesus tells us, and expects us, to love others. His point here, however, is this: We must love and treasure Jesus more than those closest to us, even if that means alienation from them because of Christ.

Several years ago, I was preaching at a rescue mission on the cost of following Christ. I noticed the disbelief on my hearers' faces as I said, "Now, who wants to follow Jesus?" This is my reason for writing this booklet. I don't claim to have it all figured out, but in my opinion, we have missed it! I have said over and over again that we just have not understood what it means to follow Jesus. What about you? Have you understood? As we observed in the last chapter, repentance and faith are the requirements to enter the narrow gate, but it is not easy. As Ryle said, "Hence arises the unspeakable importance of 'counting the cost.'" Now that we have a clearer picture of what following Christ might look like, we can better answer the question, "Which way are *we* traveling?

CHAPTER 5

THE NARROW WAY TO HEAVEN IS PAVED WITH JOYFUL SUFFERING

*I*n brief, Christians are triumphant and joyous when they suffer for the name of Jesus.

— SIMON J. KISTEMAKER

THE REALITY OF SUFFERING

Having already established that the narrow gate of Matthew 7:13 is entered by repentance and faith, and understanding the cost of following Jesus in faith, we must now turn to Jesus' words in Matthew 7:14: "Difficult is the way which leads to life, and there are few who find it." While not every Christian will suffer to the same degree, the reality is that the *few* devoted followers on the narrow way will suffer nonetheless.

In Romans 8:35 the apostle Paul listed seven types of suffering Christians might experience. Yet, he assured us that no matter how difficult, these afflictions can never separate us from the love of Christ.

Tribulation – The word has the idea of afflictions that cause pressures. These are not merely the pressures of daily living but those pressures that come upon Christians because of their union with Christ. Jesus assured us that we will have tribulations, and Paul affirmed that tribulations will pave the narrow way to heaven. "We must through many tribulations enter the kingdom of God" (Acts 14:22).

Distress—Distress is similar to tribulation but conveys the meaning of "narrowness of room."[10] Paul wrote, "For we do not want you to be ignorant, brethren, of our trouble which came to us in Asia: that we were burdened beyond measure, above strength, so that we despaired even of life" (2 Corinthians 1:8). Christians sometimes find themselves distressed by circumstances that leave them with the feeling of no escape.

Persecution – Followers of Christ are harassed and persecuted, emotionally and physically, even to the point of death. An older Russian pastor once said of persecution, "The sun *always* comes up in the east. It happens every morning … For us, persecution is like the sun coming up in the east. It happens all the time. It's the way things are. There is nothing unusual or unexpected about it. Persecution for our faith has always been—and probably always will be—a normal part of life."[11] *Every* Christian will experience persecution to some degree, for Jesus said, "If they persecuted Me, they will also persecute you" (John 15:20).

Famine – Famine refers to a lack of food and the resulting hunger. Speaking of the end times, Jesus warned, "For nation will rise against nation, and kingdom against kingdom. And there will be *famines*, pestilences, and earthquakes in various places" (Matthew 24:7, emphasis mine). Paul wrote to the Corinthians of times he suffered "in weariness and toil, in sleeplessness often, in *hunger* and thirst, in fastings often, in cold and nakedness" (2 Corinthians 11:27, emphasis mine). There may be times when we have an inadequate supply of food.

Nakedness – Having a lack of clothing may be hard for us to imagine. But others are not so fortunate. Jesus affirmed the real possibility of Christians finding themselves without clothing. When speaking of the judgment of the sheep and goats, He said, "I was naked and you clothed Me" (Matthew 25:36). Sometimes believers find themselves without proper clothing.

Peril – This term simply refers to any and all dangers. Again, Paul spoke of being "in journeys often, in perils of waters, in perils of robbers, in perils of my own countrymen, in perils of the Gentiles, in perils in the city, in perils in the wilderness, in perils in the sea, in perils among false brethren" (2 Corinthians 11:26).

Sword – The word *sword* here speaks of death. For some, following Christ leads to martyrdom. "Now about that time Herod the king stretched out his hand to harass some from the church. Then he killed James the brother of John with the sword" (Acts 12:1-2).

Christians everywhere bear witness to the reality of suffering. Jesus said, "Difficult is the way which leads to life" (Matthew 7:14). Such suffering, however, is not meaningless.

THE PURPOSE OF SUFFERING

Is there purpose in our suffering? This is a question probably every suffering Christian asks at some point. The answer is a wholehearted yes! Scripture reveals that God has chosen and predestined a people who will be "conformed to the image of His Son" (Romans 8:29). So, God uses suffering to produce in us a Christlike character. "And not only that, but we also glory in tribulations, knowing that tribulation produces perseverance; and perseverance, character; and character, hope" (Romans 5:3-4). Note what Paul said flows from tribulations.

> *Perseverance (endurance)* – When afflictions squeeze us to the point we think there is no escape and the pressures are so relentless we are tempted to lose heart, we keep going by the enabling power of the Holy Spirit. Jesus said, "And you will be hated by all for My name's sake. But he who endures to the end will be saved" (Matthew 10:22).

> *Character* – As we endure tribulations, we develop Christlike character. Isaiah records, "Behold, I have refined you, but not as silver; I have tested you in the furnace of affliction" (Isaiah 48:10). When we pass the test, our character is approved.

> *Hope* – Once our character is approved through the fiery furnace of life, hope soars. We rejoice in hope because love has been poured into our hearts by the Holy Spirit (Romans 5:5).

Suffering is indeed purposeful because of what it produces: endurance, character, and hope. And the end result of these is Christlikeness. Therefore, we can rejoice in suffering.

REJOICE IN SUFFERING?

Chapters 5 and 8 of Romans have brought me through many difficult times. I have both sections highlighted in my Bible, signifying their importance. Along with the other benefits that flow from being justified by faith—forgiveness and peace, access to the throne of grace, security in Christ, and confident hope—Paul now adds joyful suffering to the list: "And not only that, but we also glory in tribulations" (Romans 5:3). Once we see that our suffering is a purposeful gift from God to make us more like Christ, we can truly rejoice in it. Yes, the pain is real; but the way to heaven is paved with joyful suffering. Other texts also stress this rejoicing in suffering.

Blessed are those who are persecuted for righteousness' sake, for theirs is the kingdom of heaven. Blessed are you when they revile and persecute you, and say all kinds of evil against you falsely for My sake. *Rejoice and be exceedingly glad*, for great is your reward in heaven, for so they persecuted the prophets who were before you.

– MATTHEW 5:10-12 (EMPHASIS MINE)

And they [the Jewish council] agreed with him [Gamaliel], and when they had called for the apostles and beaten them, they commanded that they should not speak in the name of Jesus, and let them go. So they departed from the presence of the council, *rejoicing that they were counted worthy to suffer shame for His name.*

– ACTS 5:40-41 (EMPHASIS MINE)

Beloved, do not think it strange concerning the fiery trial which is to try you, as though some strange thing happened to you; but *rejoice* to the extent that you partake of Christ's sufferings, that when His glory is revealed, you may also be *glad with exceeding joy.*

– 1 PETER 4:12-13 (EMPHASIS MINE)

41

I sometimes find myself praying as if my suffering were a "strange" thing. But the Holy Spirit always reminds me of what Peter wrote: "Beloved, do not think it strange concerning the fiery trial which is to try you." In fact, when we suffer *rightly* (like the persecuted prophets), we actually "partake of Christ's sufferings." In other words, when we encounter tribulations because of our faithfulness to Christ, we participate in His suffering. Hence, we can, "rejoice and be exceedingly glad." Then, our suffering doesn't seem "strange" at all.

Suffering is, in fact, a reality. "In the world you will have tribulation," Jesus said (John 16:33). Whatever you are facing (or will face), you can be sure your suffering is not meaningless but purposeful, for your loving Father is intimately involved, step-by-step, with every detail of your life (Psalm 139:16). Therefore, you can "glory in tribulations" because of what they produce—endurance, character, and hope—conforming you to Christ's glorious image. When you encounter difficulties on the narrow way, remember to "rejoice and be exceedingly glad, for great is your reward in heaven."

CHAPTER 6

FROM SUFFERING TO GLORY

*P*erhaps no truth is so glaringly absent from the understanding of most Christians than the truth, and the implications thereof, that this world is not our home. When it finally settles into the heart and mind of the believer that we are "aliens and strangers in the world" (1 Pet. 2:11; cf. also Heb. 11:13; 1 Pet. 1:1), many things change. Our present sufferings will be viewed against a backdrop of future glory that relegates today's difficulties to insignificance by comparison.

– KENNETH BOA AND WILLIAM KRUIDENIER

JOINT HEIRS

One of the wonderful truths of the Christian faith is the doctrine of adoption, whereby we become children of our heavenly Father. John wrote, "But as many as received Him, to them He gave the right to become *children of God*, to those who believe in His name" (John 1:12, emphasis mine). And Paul stated, "But when the fullness of the time had come, God sent forth His Son, born of a woman, born under the law, to redeem those who were under the law, that we might receive the adoption as sons" (Galatians 4:4-5). Where we once were "sons of disobedience" (Ephesians 2:2) and "children of wrath" (Ephesians 2:3), now, by the sovereign grace of God, the work of redemption through the cross of Christ, and the ministry of the Holy Spirit, we have been set free from the law of sin and death and have become "children of God." Therefore, Paul writes, "And if children, then heirs—heirs of God and joint heirs with Christ" (Romans 8:17). In other words, we are under His loving care, provisions, and protection now, as we cry out "Abba, Father" and look forward to sharing in His future promises, blessings, and riches. Praise God! Hallelujah! But, hold on! What did Paul then write? Provided we suffer with Him? What?

PROOF THAT WE ARE JOINT HEIRS

It may seem strange that Paul would insert suffering as a proof of our inheritance, but the Holy Spirit moved him to write this truth so that when we do share in His suffering, we might be encouraged.

We were on a mission trip in Bucharest, Romania, where my dear friend Ninel Lazar and his wonderful family live. While there we were invited to the home of some beautiful Gypsy believers. The Gypsies suffer persecution because they are considered untrustworthy and thieves. And the Christians among them are even persecuted by their own people, who consider them traitors. After fellowship and singing, I taught for a few minutes, seeking to encourage them with this great biblical proof that we have become God's children: "And if children, then heirs—heirs of God and joint heirs with Christ, *if indeed we suffer with Him*" (Romans 8:17, emphasis mine).

Often we talk about the evidence, or signs, of a true believer (for example, fruit of the Spirit, a bold witness, love for the Scriptures, love for others, obedience). Amazingly, suffering gives evidence that we have been adopted into our loving Father's family. The topic of suffering shouldn't be avoided in our teaching. When we view suffering rightly (and can, in fact, rejoice in it), it gives proof that God is at work in our lives, conforming us to His glorious image, and that we share in His inheritance. But when we are tempted to grow weary, Paul gives another wonderful truth.

SUFFERING IS MOMENTARY

I think it would be safe to say the Holy Spirit has encouraged many weary Christians (including me) on the narrow way of life with this one verse: "For I consider that the sufferings of this present time are not worthy to be compared with the glory which shall be revealed in us" (Romans 8:18). I can't begin to tell you how often these words of Paul have encouraged me to continue in the faith. This is another verse we should highlight and put to memory. What stands out first is the "sufferings of this present time." Paul came to the conclusion that a few years of suffering on this earth is short and worth it. Elsewhere, Paul said, "Our light affliction ... is but for a moment" (2 Corinthians 4:17). That is, whatever people may say or do to us, these light afflictions not only serve a purpose but also are momentary. Therefore, by God's grace, "We are more than conquerors through Him who loved us" (Romans 8:37). Indeed, there is no comparison between our present suffering and our future glory.

FUTURE GLORY

What actually awaits us that so exceeds the worst of our sufferings that the two cannot even be compared? What did Paul mean at the end of Romans 8:17, when he wrote, "That we may also be glorified together"? And to what was he referring in verse 18, when he spoke of "the glory which shall be revealed in us"? And what did he have in mind when he told the Corinthians that our light affliction "is working for us a far more exceeding and eternal weight of glory" (2 Corinthians 4:17)? This all sounds really great, but what does it mean? It means our present sufferings can't even begin to compare to what will take place when our Lord returns. We are going to have a resurrected, glorified body.

> Jesus was the first to be raised from the dead to a glorified existence no longer subject to death as the punishment for sin (Acts 26:23). When He returns to this world He will raise His servants to a resurrection life like His own (1 Corinthians 15:20–23; 2 Corinthians 5:1–5; Philippians 3:20–21). He will, indeed, raise the whole human race from the dead; but those who are not His will be raised for condemnation (John 5:29) and subject to the "second death" for their sins (Revelation 2:11; 21:8). Christians alive at His coming will at that instant undergo a marvelous transformation.[12]

Those of us who endure suffering and shame for following Christ are joint heirs with Him; and when Christ returns, we will receive a "marvelous transformation"—the promise of a glorified body, free from weakness and sin. Hence, we will forever worship and serve our Lord Jesus Christ. We also will be united with our loved ones and friends who have died in Christ. And as if that weren't enough, when Christ returns, He will make all things new.

> Now I saw a new heaven and a new earth, for the first heaven and the first earth had passed away. Also there was no more sea. Then I, John, saw the holy city, New Jerusalem, coming down out of heaven from God, prepared as a bride adorned for her husband. And I heard a loud voice from

heaven saying, "Behold, the tabernacle of God is with men, and He will dwell with them, and they shall be His people. God Himself will be with them and be their God. And God will wipe away every tear from their eyes; there shall be no more death, nor sorrow, nor crying. There shall be no more pain, for the former things have passed away." Then He who sat on the throne said, "Behold, I make all things new." And He said to me, "Write, for these words are true and faithful." And He said to me, "It is done! I am the Alpha and the Omega, the Beginning and the End. I will give of the fountain of the water of life freely to him who thirsts. He who overcomes shall inherit all things, and I will be his God and he shall be My son.

— REVELATION 21:1-7

Even though we are "aliens and strangers" in the world, we have been adopted into our heavenly Father's family. We endure joyful suffering and shame for our Lord Jesus Christ, proving that we are joint heirs with Him. But our momentary suffering, which does have a purpose, cannot be compared to the glory that awaits us: a future inheritance, a glorified body, and a new heaven and earth. The narrow way is indeed paved with joyful suffering, but that suffering leads to glory!

CHAPTER 7

THE DECEPTIONS OF MANY TRAVELING THE BROAD WAY

*F*or thirty-three years I was convinced I was a Christian on my way to heaven. A year before I was truly saved, three Christians knocked on my door to share the gospel. As always, I was drinking when I invited them in, but I will never forget what took place over the next few minutes. They first asked me if I knew Jesus Christ as my Lord and Savior, and with confidence I said yes. Satisfied with my Christian lingo, they proceeded to talk with my two buddies for the next thirty minutes. Sadly, although I gave them the right answers, I was as lost as my two friends. There was no denying myself, no cross, no abandonment to His lordship, no losing of my life. My life was easy with a sprinkle of religion. But I was deceived like most people who say they believe in Jesus.

– CHUCK HAYES

THEIR DECEPTIVE DISCERNMENT

Where you find deceptive belief, you will most likely find false prophets leading people down the broad way. Jesus said, "Beware of false prophets, who come to you in sheep's clothing, but inwardly they are ravenous wolves" (Matthew 7:15). Scripture everywhere warns of false prophets and false teachers (see Jeremiah 23; Ezekiel 13; 2 Peter; Jude). While their teachings and tactics may vary, we will address them simply as people who claim to speak for God but instead lead others astray by their false doctrine and worldly way of life.

False teachers promote the wide path that inevitably leads themselves and others to destruction. Jesus said of such people in His day, "But woe to you, scribes and Pharisees, hypocrites! For you shut up the kingdom of heaven against men; for you neither go in yourselves, nor do you allow those who are entering to go in" (Matthew 23:13). What makes false teachers so dangerous and deceptive is that they come in "sheep's clothing." In other words, they are hypocrites masquerading as true shepherds. Matthew Henry offers some insight.

> Every hypocrite is a goat in sheep's clothing; not only not a sheep, but the worst enemy the sheep has, that comes not but to tear and devour, to scatter the sheep (John 10:12), to drive them from God, and from one another, into crooked paths.[13]

One way these ravenous wolves "tear and devour" others is by denying essential, nonnegotiable truths of the Christian faith such as the authority of Scripture, the person and work of Christ, the exclusivity of Christ, the Trinity, and the doctrine of justification by faith. There are some matters we can agree to disagree on, but these first-tier doctrines are not to be tampered with—ever! In the end, false teachers deny what cannot be denied and speak and write their own twisted interpretations, which are fueled by traditions, hermeneutical errors, and, yes, even demons. "Now the

Spirit expressly says that in latter times some will depart from the faith, giving heed to deceiving spirits and doctrines of demons" (1 Timothy 4:1). The bottom line is they preach another Jesus (2 Corinthians 11:4; Galatians 1:6-10)!

What naturally flows from doctrinal errors is a worldly way of life. Jude warns, "It is these who cause divisions, worldly people, devoid of the Spirit" (Jude 19, ESV). False teachers love the world. They maintain an outward appearance of religiosity, but they have an appetite for money, power, and pleasure. Jesus said of the scribes and Pharisees, "Even so you also outwardly appear righteous to men, but inside you are full of hypocrisy and lawlessness" (Matthew 23:28). False teachers are without the Spirit, so their lust and desires of the mind and flesh go unchecked. Truly they are ravenous wolves who "scatter the sheep."

Sadly, false teachers fill the pulpits of churches, consume the television and social media outlets, and write books. As such, they lead many people "into crooked paths." And the many on the wide path are unable to discern the doctrinal errors and worldliness of the false teachers, because they themselves also are deceived.

THEIR DECEPTIVE BELIEF

What we also notice about the many on the broad way is that they *believe*. Jesus said, "Not everyone who says to Me, 'Lord, Lord,' shall enter the kingdom of heaven" (Matthew 7:21). Scripture is full of examples of people who *believed* but were not saved. We find several such examples in the gospel of John.

> Now when He was in Jerusalem at the Passover, during the feast, many believed in His name when they saw the signs which He did. But Jesus did not commit Himself to them,

because He knew all men, and had no need that anyone should testify of man, for He knew what was in man.

— JOHN 2:23-25

Jesus had just turned water into wine at the wedding in Cana of Galilee (John 2:1-12) and forcefully cleansed the temple of those doing business there (vv. 13-17). The text then tells us, "Many believed in His name when they saw the signs which He did." Although they believed, Scripture reveals that theirs wasn't saving belief; and this is why "Jesus did not commit Himself to them."

Elsewhere John records, "As He spoke these words, many believed in Him" (John 8:30). Here Jesus had been speaking of His departure and warning His hearers that they would die in their sins unless they believed in Him (v. 24). He said, "And He who sent Me is with Me. The Father has not left Me alone, for I always do those things that please Him" (v. 29). Then we read, "Many believed in Him." However, as we read on through the text, it becomes clear that the many who *believed* wanted to kill Him (v. 37)! They didn't produce good works as Abraham did (v. 39); and even though they claimed God was their Father(v. 41), Jesus told them, "You are of your father the devil" (v. 44). Wow!

As we can see from just these two examples, many believed in Jesus in some manner but were deceived. And it is no different today. What is frightening is that such people, then and now, are convinced Jesus is their Lord.

> When one compares the great numbers of people today who cavalierly identify themselves as Christians yet never consider the claims of Christ, one shudders to realize how deadly such deception remains.[14]

A person can claim that Jesus is Lord and apparently even do extraordinary wonders in His name and yet hear Jesus declare, "I never knew you" (Matthew 7:22-23). Is that not one of the most fearful texts in all of Scripture? I personally know that one can *believe* and be deceived. The faith I claimed to have had was dead because I didn't do the will of God.

THEIR DECEPTIVE WAY OF LIFE (DISOBEDIENCE)

Those many who claim to believe in Christ but are deceived are characterized by their disobedience to the Father's will. Jesus said they hear His words but do not do them (Matthew 7:26). Because their belief is deceptive, what naturally follows is a deceptive way of life. That is, they are not doers of the word (James 1:22)! When one said that Jesus' mother and brothers desired to speak with Him, He responded, "Here are My mother and My brothers! For whoever does the will of My father in heaven is My brother and sister and mother" (Matthew 12:49-50).

God's will is not a mystery.

> I beseech you therefore, brethren, by the mercies of God, that you present your bodies a living sacrifice, holy, acceptable to God, which is your reasonable service. And do not be conformed to this world, but be transformed by the renewing of your mind, that you may prove what is that good and acceptable and perfect will of God.
>
> – ROMANS 12:1-2

> For this is the will of God, your sanctification: that you should abstain from sexual immorality.
>
> – 1 THESSALONIANS 4:3

In everything give thanks; for this is the will of God in Christ Jesus for you.

— 1 THESSALONIANS 5:18

For this is the will of God, that by doing good you may put to silence the ignorance of foolish men.

— 1 PETER 2:15

Therefore let those who suffer according to the will of God commit their souls to Him in doing good, as to a faithful Creator.

— 1 PETER 4:19

God has not left us in the dark in regard to His will. The above Scriptures (as well as the Sermon on the Mount) by no means exhaust the entirety of God's known will, but I think you get the picture. Jesus said, "But why do you call Me 'Lord, Lord,' and not do the things which I say?" (Luke 6:46). What defines the many on the broad way is their practice of "lawlessness" (Matthew 7:23). Again, James offers a warning to those who think belief without obedience is sufficient.

But be doers of the word, and not hearers only, deceiving yourselves.

— JAMES 1:22

THEIR DECEPTIVE WAY OF LIFE (ALWAYS AT EASE)

We observed in earlier chapters the cost of following Jesus. That great cost is something genuine Christians joyfully accept. Apart from Christ, however, people normally desire easy and comfortable living; they want to preserve their lives, not surrender them. Asaph observes, "Behold, these are the ungodly, who are always at ease; they increase in riches" (Psalm 73:12). It's amazing, isn't it? When we think of the ungodly, inevitably the worst of the worst fill our thoughts. We think of murderers and pedophiles. Rarely, if ever, do we think of people "who are always at ease." But Jesus said, "For whoever desires to save his life will lose it" (Mark 8:35). Like the false teachers, those who profess to be Christians but don't obey Christ are "always at ease." They are bent on saving their lives instead of abandoning them for the glory of our Lord.

I was leading a Bible study several years ago, and we were discussing the cost of following Christ. The next time we met, a man in the class said, "I don't want to cause any problems, but THIS IS MY LIFE." As you can imagine, my face said it all. This man was offended that Jesus would demand such loyalty and devotion. So it is with all those who are on the broad way. But Jesus says, "For whoever is ashamed of Me and My words in this adulterous and sinful generation, of him the Son of Man also will be ashamed when He comes in the glory of His Father with the holy angels" (Mark 8:38). If people are offended when they hear what Jesus requires of His followers, they only give evidence that they are ashamed of Him and His words.

Whereas the narrow way that leads to life is full of difficulties, the broad way is just the opposite. This is precisely why so many choose this popular way of easy believism; it requires nothing and promises ease. Tragically, the deception of this way of life leads to destruction.

THEIR DECEPTIVE END

The ultimate end of those who are so deceived is destruction. Jesus said, "For wide is the gate and broad is the way that leads to destruction, and there are many who go in by it" (Matthew

7:13). The many who continue traveling the wide path will be cast into the lake of fire (Revelation 20:15), where they will be "utterly consumed with terrors" (Psalm 73:19) and experience "weeping and gnashing of teeth" (Matthew 8:12). While they *believe* in Jesus, they are duped by the false prophets so that they disobey the Lord's will and seek a life of ease. Tragically, they are blinded to the coming day of wrath.

> For the great day of His wrath has come, and who is able to stand?
>
> — REVELATION 6:17

A Closing Word

*T*he words of our Lord confront each and every one of us with the fact that there are only two ways. Therefore, we all should step back, take a deep breath, and honestly examine ourselves as to which way we are traveling: the narrow way that leads to eternal life or the broad way that leads to destruction.

To enter the narrow gate, you must recognize that you are "poor in spirit"—that you are spiritually bankrupt, without hope and without God—and you must repent of your sins and believe that Jesus Christ's death on the cross was sufficient to save you. However, salvation is not easy; you must count the cost! To follow Jesus on His terms is to joyfully take up your cross daily and follow Him, bearing suffering and shame to some degree and possibly even a martyr's death. Please do not misunderstand me. This is not a "martyr's complex" or a meritorious work but the reality of following Christ. Jesus said if you are unwilling to do this, you cannot be His disciple (Luke 14:27). The narrow way to heaven is paved with joyful suffering! But that momentary suffering, which has a purpose, leads to glory!

Yet some do not believe Jesus is enough. They think works

must be added to complete the formula for eternal life: Jesus + ____ = salvation. To make matters worse, their inability to discern the errors of false teachers further blinds them to the truth of the narrow gate. They see only the popular, funny, and worldly teachers and are oblivious to their doctrinal errors. For others, the cost is simply too high to abandon the broad way. They are content to believe in a Jesus who wants them to be happy, healthy, and wealthy.

Many, like Formalist and Hypocrisy in Bunyan's Christian allegory, find themselves on the broad way. I ought to know, I spent most of my adult life there. In a day when numbers, prosperity, and outward manifestations define much of evangelicalism, it's not surprising to find so many of our family, friends, and neighbors unwilling to search the Scriptures to see if these things are so. Jesus set the bar so high that only the few, by God's grace, will, in fact, enter the narrow gate and travel the narrow way, fully accepting that "through many tribulations we must enter the kingdom of God." The stakes are high. Heaven and hell hang in the balance. Which way are *we* traveling?

NOTES

1.   John Bunyan, *The Pilgrim's Progress from This World to That Which Is to Come; Delivered under the Similitude of a Dream*, ed. Joanne Panettieri (Amazon Digital Services, 2013), Kindle Edition, 26.

2.   John Gill, *John Gill's Exposition of the Bible*, Biblestudytools.com.

3.   William Hendriksen, *Exposition of the Gospel According to John*, New Testament Commentary (Grand Rapids: Baker, 1983), 69.

4.   John Philips, *Exploring the Gospel of John* (Grand Rapids: Kregel, 2001), 26.

5.   Leon Morris, "Propitiation," in *The New Bible Dictionary*, ed. J. D. Douglas (Grand Rapids: Eerdmans, 1962), 1046.

6.   C. H. Spurgeon, "'Faith and Repentance Inseparable,' A Sermon (No. 460) Delivered on Sunday Morning, July 13, 1862, by C. H. Spurgeon, At the Metropolitan Tabernacle, Newington," Spurgeon.org.

7.   Christian Apologetics & Research Ministry, "Faith," in "Dictionary of Theology," http://carm.org/dictionary-faith

8.   James *Strong, The New Strong's Expanded Dictionary of Bible Words* (Nashville: Nelson, 2001), 1451.

9.   David Platt, *Radical: Taking Back Your Faith from the American Dream* (Colorado Springs: Multnomah, 2010), 10.

10. James Strong, *King James New Strong's Exhaustive Concordance* (Nashville: Nelson, 2001), 83.

11. Nik Ripken and Greg Lewis, *The Insanity of God: A True Story of Faith Resurrected* (Nashville: B&H Publishing, 2013), Kindle Edition, 161.

12. R. C. Sproul, ed., *The Reformation Study Bible: English Standard Version* (Lake Mary, FL: Ligonier, 2005), 1666.

13. Matthew Henry, *Matthew Henry's Commentary on the Whole Bible: Complete,* Vol. 5: Matthew to John (Peabody, MA: Hendrickson, 2009), 76.

14. Craig S. Keener, *Matthew,* The IVP New Testament Commentary Series (Downers Grove, IL: InterVarsity, 1997), 163.

www.ingramcontent.com/pod-product-compliance
Lightning Source LLC
Chambersburg PA
CBHW060724030426
42337CB00017B/3004